The Secret For Children

WRITTEN AND ILLUSTRATED
BY
CINDY DEHAVEN

Copyright © 2012 Cindy DeHaven
All rights reserved.

ISBN: 1419667408

ISBN 13: 9781419667404

LCCN: 2010913738

North Charleston, South Carolina

For Harry...
I love you every day

As you wake up each
morning you have the gift
of another day
Smile, open your eyes, the
sun is lighting your way.

Give your family hugs and
kisses too
They are helping you grow,
and loving you.

Take care of your pets and
enjoy when they play
They love to share your
joy every day.

Cherish the seasons
as they come and go
Flowers, sun, leaves, and snow.

At school thank your teacher
for helping you today
Learning is a gift that you will
teach someday.

Spend time with your
friends, be sure to laugh
and play
Tell them you like them and
have fun with your day.

Love yourself and all you can do
And be ready because others will too.

And if something doesn't go your way
You are the one who can change your bad day.

You can make all of your
dreams come true
Be proud and grateful
just to be you.

And when someone asks why you are smiling, say... "I know the secret to having a great day!"

Thank you for today,
thank you for tonight

Thank you for tomorrow,
and the rest of my life.

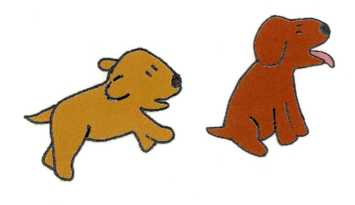

Cindy DeHaven learned the importance of sustaining the right attitude to achieve her goals, and she's grateful for all her accomplishments. The author passes her enthusiasm and zest for life on to her son, Harry, each and every day. They live in Haslett, Michigan with their two dogs.

Made in the USA
Las Vegas, NV
20 September 2022